LEARN SHAPES and COLORS

Library of Congress in Publication Data

Reed, Giles.
  Learn shapes and colors with the Munch Bunch.

  Summary: The activities of the Munch Bunch provide
practice in recognizing nine colors and nine geometric
shapes.
  1. Geometry—Juvenile literature. 2. Color—Juvenile
literature. [1. Size and shape. 2. Color] I. Mitson,
Angela, ill. II. Title.
QA447.R43 1981   535.6   81-12046
ISBN 0-86625-079-4   AACR2

Rourke Publications, Inc.
Windermere, FL   32786

RED, YELLOW and BLUE
The three primary colors are red, yellow and blue.

RED

Tom Tomato is red. He has dropped a can of red paint on Pete Pepper's head.

YELLOW

The Banana Bunch and Lucy Lemon
are yellow.

BLUE

Blue is the color of the sea. It is also the color of Peanut's hat.

ORANGE is made by mixing red with yellow.

Pedro Orange and Casper Carrot are orange.

 GREEN is made by mixing blue with yellow.
Scruff Gooseberry is green. He is
frightening Emma Apple with his worm.

PURPLE is made by mixing red with blue.

The Munch Bunch are watching a show.

The stage has purple curtains.

BROWN is made by mixing yellow with blue and red.

Spud is giving Wally Walnut a ride.

BLACK

The Banana Bunch and Pedro Orange

live in black boots.

WHITE

All the Munch Bunch enjoy playing in the snow.

CIRCLE

How many circular things can you see?

I can see some circular wheels.

OVAL

How many ovals can you see?

I can see some oval eggs.

SQUARE

How many square things can you see?

I can see a square picture on the wall.

TRIANGLE

How many triangles can you see?

I can see a triangular hat.

RECTANGLE

How many rectangles can you see?

I can see a rectangular box.

STAR

OCTAGON

HEXAGON

DIAMOND

circle · oval · square

rectangle · triangle

Professor Peabody is teaching some of the Munch Bunch the shapes we have seen so far.

 **A RED CIRCLE**

A YELLOW OVAL

A BLUE SQUARE

AN ORANGE TRIANGLE

A GREEN RECTANGLE

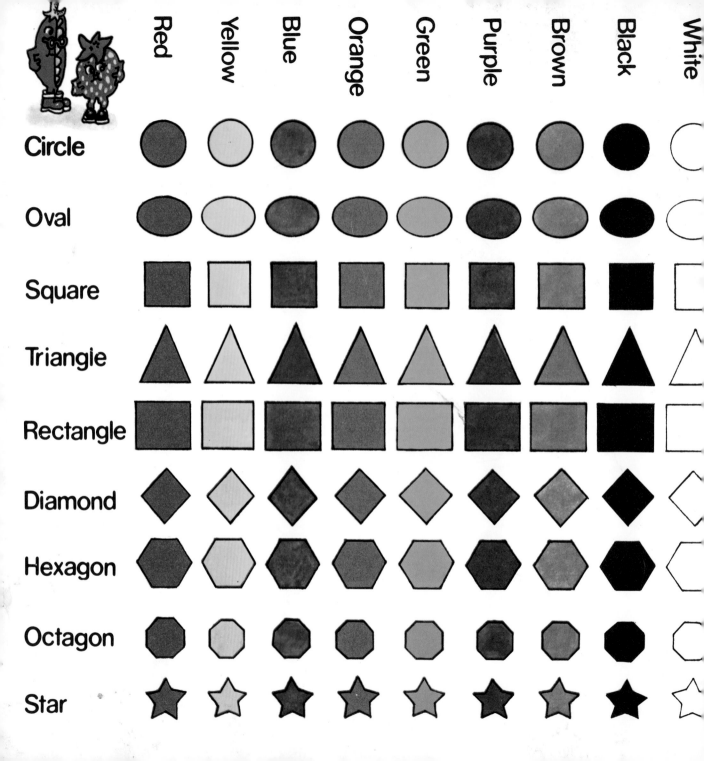